SoulVibes: Love, Lessons, and my Sadguru's Grace

Love Everyone Through Your Heart

Keshav Velhal

India | USA | UK

Dedication

Om Ganeshaya Namah

I begin this dedication with a prayer to Lord Ganesha, the remover of obstacles and the bestower of wisdom. May His divine blessings pave the way for love, peace, and clarity in all our journeys.

This book, Poems on Love by the Grace of My Sadguru, is dedicated with deep gratitude and love to those who have shaped my journey.

To my beloved parents, whose endless support and love have been my constant strength, grounding me through every phase of life.

To my revered Sadguru, Swami Makarandnath of the Nath Sampradaya, whose wisdom and grace continue to guide my every step. It is through His divine influence that I have found the path to love and devotion.

To Dr. Radhakrishnan Pillai, my mentor and
guru, whose teachings have profoundly inspired
me to embark on this writing journey and
whose guidance has shaped my understanding
of life and love.

To my dear friends, Sagar and Swarnim, for
their unwavering encouragement, belief in me,
and constant companionship through every
chapter of this journey.

This collection is a humble offering of love and
gratitude to all of you.

Acknowledgment

This book would not have been possible without the love, guidance, and inspiration of many wonderful souls who have touched my life. I am deeply grateful to each of you for your support and presence in my journey.

First and foremost, I would like to express my heartfelt gratitude to my parents, whose unwavering love and constant encouragement have been the foundation of everything I do. Their belief in me has been my greatest source of strength.

To my revered Sadguru, Swami Makarandnath of the Nath Sampradaya, I owe a debt of gratitude for his divine grace and wisdom, which have profoundly shaped my understanding of love and life. His teachings have been the guiding light behind this collection.

I am deeply thankful to Dr. Radhakrishnan Pillai, my mentor and guru, whose teachings and guidance have inspired me to put my thoughts into words. His wisdom has been instrumental in shaping my journey as a writer.

To my cherished friends, Sagar and Swarnim, your unwavering encouragement and belief in me have been a constant source of motivation. Your friendship has been a cornerstone in my life, and for that, I am forever grateful.

I would also like to acknowledge the love and devotion that flows through the spiritual and divine forms celebrated in these poems—the nine forms of Durga, the eternal love of Krishna and Radha, the sacred bonds of Ram and Sita, Shiva and Parvathi, the grace of Lord Ganesha, and the love of Allah. These divine influences have enriched my understanding of love in its highest forms.

Finally, I extend my gratitude to my pets, whose pure and unconditional love has brought joy and peace into my life. Their simple affection reminds me daily of the power of love in its purest form.

To all who have supported me in this journey, whether directly or indirectly, I thank you from the bottom of my heart. This book is a reflection of the love that surrounds us all, and I am humbled to share it with the world.

Keshav Velhal

Preface

This book is a heartfelt collection of poems that explores the boundless nature of love in its many forms. Inspired by the grace and wisdom of my Sadguru, Swami Makarandnath, this book is a reflection of the deep connections that shape our lives and the divine presence that binds them together.

At its core, this collection celebrates love in all its beautiful manifestations: the unconditional love of parents and grandparents, the unbreakable bond of best friends, and the sacred love of the gods and goddesses revered in our spiritual heritage. Each poem is a journey into the love that transcends time and space, both human and divine.

You will find here the love of Durga in her nine forms, the tender devotion between Krishna and Radha, the eternal bond of Ram and Sita, and the cosmic union of Shiva and Parvathi. The love of Lord Ganesha, the remover of obstacles, is celebrated as much as the love for Allah, whose mercy envelops all. Even the simple yet profound love of pets, who offer us pure affection without condition, finds a place in these verses.

This book is not just a tribute to these forms of love but also a reminder that love is the essence of life itself. Whether it be the familial love that shapes our foundation or the divine love that guides our spirit, love is the force that connects us to each other and to the universe.

I hope these poems bring you closer to the love that resides in your heart, and I humbly offer this collection to the reader as a celebration of love in its purest form.

With the grace of my Sadguru and the love of those dear to me, this book has come into being. May it resonate with your soul and inspire love in all aspects of your life.

Keshav Velhal

Born from Love, Born of Light

You are born from nothing, yet everything you are,
From stardust, from whispers of light from afar.
Your parents make love, their hearts intertwined,
In that union, your spark begins to shine.

Your desire, the divine, and your mind all align,
A sacred dance, a cosmic design.
The divine element begins to grow,
In your mother's womb, life starts to flow.

From love, you arrive, a gift to this earth,
A radiant soul with infinite worth.
You take birth from the heart of your mother,
A bond like no other, stronger than any other.

As soon as you're born, you're her heart's
delight,
A love that grows, both gentle and bright.
And as you are born, you're your father's
strength,
A love that stretches through infinite length.

You're born from love, pure and true,
The essence of life, the eternal you.
In every breath, in every tear,
The love you came from will always be near.

So remember, dear soul, as you grow and
ascend,
You are born from love—love that will never
end.

The Infinite Love of Parents

Understanding a parent's love is no easy feat,
It's a bond that runs deep, though not always
sweet.
You cling to them closely until you're eleven,
They guide you, love you as gifts from heaven.

But as you enter the restless teen years,
You feel their love turns into your fears.
You think they don't get the things you
conceal,
Your secrets untold, the walls you now feel.

In your twenties, independence takes its place,
You think their worries are out of pace.
You feel self-sufficient, strong, and so free,
Why need their advice? You're who you should
be.

But as they grow old and you stay young,
Their love remains strong, their song still
unsung.
In time, you'll see that they were right,
As life unfolds, they are your guiding light.

When you have children of your own one day,
Their value becomes clear in every way.
Everyone may leave, but they'll remain,
Through joy, through hardship, through every
pain.

Their love is infinite; it never ends,
So cherish them now as life's greatest friends.
Embrace them, hug them, love them while you
can,
For their days are numbered, just like sand.

So love your parents with all your might,
For they are gods in human light.

A Mother's Infinite Love

A mother's love starts before you're born,
From the moment in her womb, you're worn.
She eats for you; her heart beats true,
Making sure life grows within you.

Connected by a cord so deep,
Her every breath, your soul does keep.
She bears the pain when you arrive,
Could you endure it and still survive?

She holds you close with tender care,
Feeds you, bathes you, smooths your hair.
A goddess, her love knows no end,
Without a thought for gender, she'll defend.

Even when you're rude, she'll forgive,
Her love for you forever will live.
As you grow, you might not see,
How much she loves and lets you be.

Do you care for her like she for you?
Her heart breaks for all you go through.
Lord Krishna said, "Once gone, none mourn for
long,
But a mother's grief is lifelong strong.

If you pass before her time,
She'll weep through heaven's endless climb.
So wipe her tears and calm her fears,
Keep her close through all the years.

Forgive her as she forgives you,
For the pain she bore to make you new.
She broke for you, endured life's strife—
32 bones, to give you life."

I shed my tears for her today,
Oh, mother, I love you in every way.
Oh, mother, I love you infinitely,
In your embrace, I find eternity.

The Silent Love of a Father

Your father loves you, even before you take your first breath,
He loves you silently, from the moment you're in the womb.
Your father loves you, even before you take your first breath,
His love is quiet, not always expressed, but ever so deep.

He is a silent lover who hides his emotions time after time,
He is a silent lover who hides his emotions time after time,
But through his actions, his care shines like a guiding light,
As you grow, he will shield you, ensuring you are always safe.

He might work long, exhausting hours under the
sun or moon,
Just to fulfill that one little wish you made
without a second thought.
He might sacrifice his comfort to bring you joy,
Choosing your happiness over his own, with
every passing day.

He could buy something simple for himself,
Yet his heart tells him to buy something for you
instead.
He might wear torn sandals, patched shoes, and
weathered clothes,
But he will always make sure you have new
ones to wear.
Oh, what love is this? A love so pure, selfless,
and true.

In your teenage years, you may think he doesn't
understand,
That he's out of touch, unaware of how the
world has changed.
But as you grow older, as you build your own
life and family,
You'll see his wisdom, his rightness, and his
unwavering strength.

A father's love is silent, but it's a fortress you
can always lean on,

He completes his duty without asking for praise
or applause.
He shields you from the storms with his love,
He shields you from the storms with his love.

Remember, as you grow strong and young,
He grows older, more fragile with each passing
year.
So take care of him, spend time with him,
Show him the love that he quietly poured into
you.

For when you are lost and the world turns
away,
He will be the one standing by your side,
holding you up.
His love is infinite, boundless, like the sky
above.
Parents are gods themselves, sent to love and
protect you,
Parents are gods themselves, sent to love and
protect you.

Love of Your Sadguru

The love of your Sadguru is infinite,
The love of your Sadguru is infinite.
When you're in trouble, you feel alone,
But he's the one who walks beside you when
you're whole.

On the beach, four footprints you see,
Yours and his, a peaceful harmony.
But in your pain, you find only two—
Guess how, guess how? He's carrying you, you
will see.

He is the guiding light, your eternal torch,
Listen to his words; never let them scorch.
Only a Sadguru will show you the way
To self-realization, where peace will stay.

None other will lead you to the truth,
Bow down to him; walk with him in life's
booth.
Surrender at his feet, let go of the chase—
Money, fame, lust—meaningless in his grace.

With your Sadguru by your side, you'll see,
It's all an illusion; nothing is meant to be.
You'll be blessed by the truth of nothingness,
Understanding at last, this is life's pure bliss.

In the end, you'll realize the greatest karma,
Is surrendering at his feet, free from all drama.
If you do, if you do, give in at last—
You'll dance in the joy of "Soham" so vast.

As I close this poem, I bow to his feet,
Hand over my lust, my ego, desires, victory, and
defeat.
My only prayer now is simple and whole—
May this body be used for his work,
And merge into his infinite soul.

The Love of a Teacher

A teacher's love, so hard to explain,
It's deep and selfless, without any gain.
You may not always see her care,
She'll teach, she'll scold, she'll even dare.
But behind it all, there's love so true,
Every word, every lesson, is just for you.

She stays up late, her mind in a race,
To learn more, so she can keep up the pace.
A thankless job, but she doesn't mind,
For her joy is in the knowledge you find.
Few return to honor her part,
But she remembers you, keeps you in her heart.

She moves from one to the next in line,
But every student, she calls "mine."
Oh, such is the love a teacher bestows,
A love that in every student grows.

So thank her, dear, with all your grace,
For she's the one who helped you find your
place.

The Love of a Best Friend

The love of a best friend knows no bounds,
In laughter, in tears, they're always around.
They'll cry with you, fight by your side,
And through every battle, with you, they'll ride.

They won't lie to you when you're going astray,
Their truth is a gift, come what may.
They'll leave their own good behind for your
sake,
With every mistake, they'll help you awake.

They'll scold you gently when you're wrong,
But cheer the loudest when you grow strong.
In moments of pain, they'll stand by your side,
And in your old age, they'll still be your guide.

With your best friend, you may have a few snaps,
But infinite memories fill in the gaps.
Whether childhood pals or new from the start,
They'll always hold a place in your heart.

Even if you wander down the wrong way,
They might walk with you, come what may.
And after a fight, they may stay mad,
But soon return with a hug, making you glad.

You may not talk for days on end,
But deep down, you know they're your friend.
So if you have such love, so rare and true,
Hold them tight, for they care deeply for you.

Their love is a treasure, a gift without compare,
And in their hearts, they'll always be there.

Hymn to Devi Shailputri

With love from Devi Shailputri, so divine,
Her blessings upon us, pure and fine.
On Navratri's first day, we bow and pray,
To the daughter of mountains, we offer our
stay.

Shailputri, the child of Shaila, strong and free,
The embodiment of Shakti's energy.
Orange is the hue we wear in her grace,
She fills our hearts with joy in every space.

She brings enthusiasm, success, and cheer,
Her blessings drive away doubt and fear.
Pray to her, chant her name with love,
Om Devī Shailaputryai Namah, to the heavens
above.

Vande Vānchhitalābhāya, adorned with the moon,
On her sacred bull, she rides so soon.
Shuladharām, Shailaputrīm, shining bright,
We honor her with devotion in the morning light.

Hymn to Devi Brahmacharini

With love from Devi Brahmacharini, so pure,
Her blessings upon us, steadfast and sure.
On Navratri's second day, we bow and pray,
To the Goddess of penance, who lights our
way.

Brahmacharini walks with grace and might,
In her right hand, a Japa mala bright,
In her left, the kamandalu she holds,
A tale of renunciation, her story unfolds.

White is her color, pure as the snow,
She brings peace and bliss, making hearts glow.
She walks barefoot, with her sacred vow,
Endowing her devotees with grace, here and
now.

Parvati once resolved to marry Shiva strong,
For 5,000 years, her penance went long.
Though gods tried to sway her heart and mind,
She stayed on her path, steady and kind.

Demons came to test her will,
But her resolve remained stronger still.
When Prakandasura attacked with might,
Her penance summoned a flood of light.

Gods Lakshmi and Saraswati came to her aid,
Yet the million demons left them dismayed.
But when her kamandalu fell to the ground,
The water washed the demons all around.

At last, her tapas caught Shiva's gaze,
He met her in disguise, testing her ways.
With every riddle, she answered so wise,
Shiva appeared, breaking her tapas in surprise.

Now we worship her, in pure devotion's flame,
Oṃ Devī Brahmacāriṇyai Namaḥ, we
proclaim.
Dadhana kara Padmabhyam, the lotus she
bears,
With akshamala, she listens to our prayers.

O Devi, bless us with peace so divine,
In every being, let your light shine.

Namastasyai, Namastasyai, we sing in her
name,
To Brahmacharini, forever the same.

Hymn to Devi Chandraghanta

With love from Devi Chandraghanta, we sing,
Her blessings to us, with grace she brings.
On Navratri's third day, we bow and pray,
For peace and prosperity to light our way.

She wears a half-moon, shaped like a bell,
Upon her forehead, her power does dwell.
Riding a tigress, fierce and bold,
With ten hands, her story is told.

Trishul, sword, and kamandalu she bears,
In her Varadamudra, she dispels our fears.
A lotus, arrow, and Dhanush in hand,
In Abhaya Mudra, she makes her stand.

Red is the color, her passion aflame,
Fearless, she fights in Shiva's name.

For every woman, she shows the way,
Strength in beauty, courage each day.

Parvati wed Shiva, their story unfolds,
Her heart remained strong, her spirit bold.
But a demon arose, Tarkasura by name,
Seeking to end Shiva's lineage and fame.

Jatukasura, with his army of bats,
Attacked Parvati, trying to strike her flat.
She stood in fear but remembered her might,
That she is Shakti, the eternal light.

In the dark, Parvati called on the moon,
Chandra Dev shone brightly, ending the gloom.
Wolves came to aid her in this fateful fight,
Bats flew away at her bell's ringing might.

With her ghanta, she struck Jatukasura down,
Wolves howled as his form hit the ground.
Her sword cut his wings; her power prevailed,
In Chandraghanta, no force could have sailed.

Shiva praised her, her strength so divine,
A lesson for all, in every line:
No woman is weak, no heart is frail,
With Shakti within, she will always prevail.

Chandraghanta shines, golden and bright,

A symbol of grace, courage, and light.
With ten hands, she blesses, dispels every fear,
In her presence, we feel her power near.

Oṃ Devī Chandraghanta Namaḥ, we cry,
In her strength and beauty, we lift our eyes
high.
Oṃ Devī Chandraghanta Namaḥ, we sing,
Her blessings upon us, forever they cling.

Hymn to Devi Kushmanda

O Devi Kushmanda, full of radiant light,
We worship your glory on the fourth day
bright.
With blessings you give, we bow down and
pray,
Your luminous smile brings life to the day.

Living within the blazing sun's core,
You create the world, and life does restore.
O Ashtabhuja Devi, with eight arms so grand,
Holding weapons and blessings in each gentle
hand.

With trident and discus, sword and the bow,
The power of your might makes evil
overthrow.
In one hand, a lotus; in another, the mace,
Your Abhaya mudra blesses all with grace.

Royal blue is the color we wear in your name,
Elegance and richness you forever proclaim.
You sit on a tiger, fierce and strong,
Guiding us right, where we belong.

Once the Sun left its place, causing dismay,
You brought it back with your fire's display.
In the heart of the Sun, you make your throne,
Giving it strength, making the universe known.

When darkness spread and lights went dim,
You created the Sun's eternal hymn.
With your power, the balance was restored,
The cosmos aligned; life was once more.

O mother of creation, Shakti divine,
The sun's glowing warmth is your eternal sign.
We worship you, Kushmanda, source of all
light,
You guide us in darkness, making everything
bright.

Om Devi Kushmanda Namah, we say,
We seek your blessings on this sacred day.
Your strength and grace we humbly adore,
O Devi Kushmanda, forevermore.

Hymn to Devi Skandamata

On the fifth day of Navratri, we seek your light,
O Devi Skandamata, fierce and bright.
You ride the lion with grace and might,
With Lord Skanda in your tender sight.

Simhasanagata Nityam, on your throne you
stay,
Padmashrita Karadvaya, with lotus in hand each
day.
Shubhadastu Sada Devi, forever you bless,
Skandamata Yashasvinim, you bring us
success.

O Mother of fire, fierce and kind,
Your blessings purify the heart and mind.
With wisdom, salvation, treasures untold,
Your grace brings power, prosperity, and gold.

Ya Devi Sarvabhuteshu, in every soul you
reside,
Ma Skandamata Rupena, in your form we
abide.
Namastasyai, Namastasyai, again we bow,
Namastasyai Namo Namah, before you now.

Worship her saying **Oṃ Devī Skandamātāyai
Namaḥ**,
Worship her saying **Oṃ Devī Skandamātāyai
Namaḥ**.

On this sacred day, dressed in a yellow hue,
We worship you, O Mother, so true.
Skandamata, O goddess divine,
In your blessings, let our spirits shine.

Worship her saying **Oṃ Devī Skandamātāyai
Namaḥ**,
Worship her saying **Oṃ Devī Skandamātāyai
Namaḥ**.

Hymn to Devi Katyayani

O Devi Katyayani, fierce and bright,
Born from flames of gods' pure might.
We worship you on the sixth day's light,
To seek your blessings, power, and sight.

Oṃ Devī Katyayani Namaḥ, we humbly say,
Oṃ Devī Katyayani Namaḥ, with hearts we
pray.

From Vamana Purana's sacred lore,
You were born from energy's core.
In Katyayana's hermitage, you came to be,
To destroy Mahishasura and set us free.

With Shiva's trident and Vishnu's disc in hand,
You received weapons from every god of the
land.
Agni's dart and Vayu's bow,
Your strength made all evils bow.

O Devi Katyayani, we honor your might,
On the Mysore hills, you fought the fight.
With a lion beneath, you fiercely rode,
To end the terror that demons sowed.

Mahishasura fell by your tender feet,
You struck him down with force so sweet.
With sword in hand, you ended his reign,
And the world rejoiced, free from pain.

Chandrahasojjvalakara, shining so bright,
Shaardulavaravahana, lion your ride of light.
Katyayani, Shubham Dadyad, grace you
bestow,
Devi Danavaghatini, destroyer of every foe.

Oṃ Devī Katyayani Namaḥ, we humbly say,
Oṃ Devī Katyayani Namaḥ, with hearts we
pray.

Raktabīja's curse you overcame,
Swallowing blood without letting it stain.
Creating nectar to rejuvenate the brave,
You helped Bhairava in victory pave.

In Tuljapur, your temple stands tall,
The Bhosales and Shivaji, on you would call.
With Bhavani's sword, you gave him might,

To protect the kingdom with righteous light.

O mother of new beginnings, full of grace,
Green we wear to evoke your embrace.
Ya Devi Sarvabhuteshu, in every heart you
stay,
Ma Katyayani Rupena, guiding our way.

Namastasyai Namastasyai, we bow to you in
prayer,
Namastasyai Namo Namah, for you are always
there.

Worship her with **Oṃ Devī Katyayani
Namaḥ**,
Worship her with **Oṃ Devī Katyayani
Namaḥ**.

Hymn to Devi Kalaratri

On the seventh day, we bow and pray,
To Maa Kalaratri, fierce and gray.
With eyes like fire, her tongue blood-red,
She walks the path where none dare tread.

Her form is dark, her soul is bold,
Her hair unbound, wild and cold.
A sword in hand, an iron hook,
In her fierce eyes, fear cannot look.

She rides a donkey through the night,
Her presence fills the heart with might.
Though terrifying to the ones who sin,
For her devotees, she shines within.

Oṃ Devī Kālarātryai Namaḥ we chant,
For her blessings we deeply grant.
To face the darkness, she stands near,
Removing all sorrow, removing all fear.

Kaal Ratrim, adorned in divine light,
Her necklace shines, like stars so bright.
With a fearless heart, we wear the gray,
Balanced, grounded, we honor this day.

She drinks the blood of demons vile,
Destroys their clones, their deadly guile.
In the darkest hour, she stands tall,
Protecting us, she saves us all.

So, on this day of Maharatri's reign,
We seek her love, forget our pain.
Oṃ Devī Kālarātryai Namaḥ, we call,
In her fearless embrace, we stand tall.

Karalvandana dhoram, Muktkeshi true,
Her blessings flow to me and you.
Kaal Ratrim, fierce and free,
May her light shine eternally.

Oṃ Devī Kālarātryai Namaḥ, we say,
With grace, we worship her on this day.

Hymn to Devi Mahagauri

On the eighth day, we worship thee,
Mahagauri, pure as the sea,
Blessings from you, so divine,
With a radiant glow that does shine.

Your beauty gleams like pearls so bright,
Bringing peace, joy, and endless light,
Flaws and fears you burn away,
Purifying souls on this blessed day.

In purple, we dress, the hue of power,
To honor your grace in this sacred hour,
You hold the trident and tambourine,
With blessings and protection, serene.

You rode the ox, majestic and fair,
To Kailash, where love's flame did flare,
Shiva beside you, sons in sight,
Together, you illuminate the night.

Om Devi Mahagauryai Namah, we chant,
Your strength and love, we humbly grant,
Bless us, Mother, with purity's gleam,
In your light, may we forever dream.

Om Devi Mahagauryai Namah ||
Om Devi Mahagauryai Namah ||

Hymn to Devi Siddhidharti

On the night of the ninth day, we praise,
Devi Siddhidharti, in your divine gaze,
Blessings from you, oh Goddess so bright,
Illuminate our hearts with your radiant light.

From the void of darkness, you brought forth
grace,
A sea of light, in this sacred space,
Mahashakti, the Supreme, gave birth to the
Three,
Brahma, Vishnu, and Shiva, in harmony.

With wisdom profound, you guided their way,
Bestowing upon them their duties to play,
Goddess of Siddhis, your powers divine,
Eight miraculous gifts, in their hearts you
entwine.

Anima, Mahima, and Garima's might,
Laghima's lightness, Prapti's endless sight,
Prakambya, Ishitva, and Vashitva's sway,
You granted them strength to fulfill their way.

Seated on a lotus, in four arms you shine,
Lotus, mace, Chakra, and conch intertwine,
You remove ignorance, bestow knowledge so
pure,
In your divine presence, our spirits endure.

Oṃ Devī Siddhidharti Namaḥ, we chant in
love,
Your blessings and guidance, sent from above,
On this sacred night, we humbly implore,
May we find in your grace, our hearts
evermore.

Oṃ Devī Siddhidharti Namaḥ,
Oṃ Devī Siddhidharti Namaḥ,
Oṃ Devī Siddhidharti Namaḥ.

The Love of a True Friend

The love of a true friend is rare and unique,
A bond so strong, no need to speak.
He stands beside you through thick and thin,
His loyalty shines; it's where friendships begin.

When you stumble and fall, he extends his
hand,
Lifts you up, helps you stand.
When you're wrong, he'll scold you firm,
But his care is deep, beyond concern.

When tears flow down, he lends his shoulder,
A comfort so warm, as the nights grow colder.
When sickness strikes, he's there to care,
A gentle touch, showing he's always aware.

And when you succeed, though quiet he seems,
From the sidelines, he cheers your dreams.

He may not praise you to your face,
But behind closed doors, your worth he'll
embrace.

When your pockets run low, he's quick to lend,
Sharing his strength, like only a friend.
Your problems become his, your struggles
shared,
In every battle, he's fully prepared.

Through life's winding path, he's by your side,
A constant companion, your trusted guide.
So my dear champ, be a friend that's true,
For in loving others, the same will come to you.

The Love of a Grandfather

The love of a grandfather is truly divine,
A bond so strong, it stands the test of time.
He holds your hand as you learn and grow,
Guiding you gently, in ways you may never
know.

With every story, he shows you life's true way,
Teaching you the wisdom that words alone can't
say.
He's walked through more years than you've
ever seen,
So listen with your heart to all that he's been.

Though his years with you may be too few,
Every moment shared is a gift so true.
Cherish his laughter, his warmth, his embrace,
For one day, these memories you'll long to
retrace.

He scolds when you stray to set you right,
But pampers you with love before the night.
In your teenage years, when the world's a haze,
He's the one who listens through all your days.

He'll talk to you on any topic at all,
From dreams to fears, he'll catch your fall.
His love knows no limits, no bounds to hold,
A treasure more precious than silver or gold.

So while he's here, hug him tight,
Sit by his side in the soft twilight.
Listen to his stories, his wisdom, his care,
For one day, you'll find he's no longer there.

But even then, his love will remain,
A part of your heart that feels no pain.
For grandfathers leave a legacy of grace,
A love that time cannot erase.

The Love of a Grandmother

Oh, the love of a grandmother, beyond
imagination,
A love so pure, it defies explanation.
She's the mother of your mother or father, it's
true,
But to her, you're the star in all she'll do.

You are her little pumpkin pie, her sweetest
delight,
In her care, everything feels so right.
She'll love you more than even her own,
For in her eyes, you are the treasure she's grown.

She'll bathe you gently, feed you with care,
Play with you, scold you, always be there.
Her love pours out in infinite ways,
Turning ordinary moments into golden days.
You are her pumpkin pie, her joy, her pride,

She'll shield you always, with love as wide as
the sky.

A friend, a guardian, with wisdom to share,
No one can love you with such tender care.
When the world feels heavy and you're feeling
small,
Her arms are the place where you'll stand tall.

She'll scold her own children if need be,
Just to ensure you're happy, wild, and free.
She'll listen to the secrets you whisper at night,
And make everything feel alright.

Her love is a force that can't be measured,
An endless ocean, a priceless treasure.
So cherish her laughter, her stories, her time,
For she'll always love you, in ways so sublime.

Take care of her, hold her close, and never let
go,
For her love is a gift that forever will grow.
In her eyes, you'll always be her pumpkin pie,
A love that's eternal, that will never say
goodbye.

So while she's here, hug her tight every day,
Her love is a blessing that will never fade away.

The Love of a Life Partner

The love of a life partner is yours to decide,
In your hands, it rests, like the ebbing tide.
How much you love, how deep you care,
Is a choice you make with moments to share.

Loving your life partner is beautifully unique,
Through highs and lows, it's not always sleek.
It's up to you how long you drag a fight,
How fast you end it and make things right.

In your shared journey, maturity will guide,
In sorrow, you should hold each other tight.
In love, you embrace with hearts so true,
In victory, stand tall, just me and you.

The balance may shift from day to day,
80/20 or 50/50, as life finds its way.
But always remember, no matter the strain,

Contribution is key, through joy and through pain.

A simple "sorry" will never cause harm,
Even if you weren't at fault, it will disarm.
It heals the heart, smooths over the strife,
And strengthens the bond of husband and wife.

For parents may leave, and children will roam,
But with your life partner, you'll find your true home.
They'll stay with you, step by step, till the end,
A lover, a confidant, your truest friend.

So cherish them deeply, hug them tight,
Pamper them with love, bring them light.
Gift them with flowers, show them your care,
For they chose to walk this journey with you,
Through every moment, till the end, to share.

The Love of Radha and Krishna

The love of Radha was so deep, she kept her
eyes closed tight,
Waiting for the day she'd see Krishna's face,
glowing in Barsana's light.
As children, they played hand in hand; she, his
sakhi, he, her friend,
In each other's company, their joy knew no end.

Krishna's flute would fill the air, and Radha
danced with grace,
Their Raas Lila, divine and pure, no words could
ever trace.
Their love was infinite, beyond all time, a bond
that never fades,
In every melody of Krishna's tune, Radha's
essence played.

Once the Lord had a headache, a pain no cure
could find,
Only the dust from Radha's feet could ease his
troubled mind.
Such was the power of their love, so selfless and
so true,
Radha gave her everything, as Krishna's heart
she knew.

When Krishna left for Mathura, her heart
shattered in pain,
Yet she loved him still, without complaint, as
though he'd never wane.
In every breath, in every tear, she felt his
presence near,
Her love was pure, unwavering, free of doubt or
fear.

They met again in dreams and thoughts, their
spirits intertwined,
For Radha's love transcended all, in body, heart,
and mind.
If one seeks to love, let it be as Radha loved her
Lord,
For in their story lies a truth, a love forever
adored.

Their love was not of mortal kind but divine,
vast, and grand,

It teaches us that to truly love, we must fully
understand.
Beyond the self, beyond the mind, beyond
what's seen or heard,
Love like Radha loved Krishna—pure, eternal,
and undeterred.

The Love of Lord Ram for Devi Sita

You made me indebted, my Lakshmi dear Sita
says Rama, with your grace so bright,
Now I need neither heaven nor its eternal light.
Ah, I am lost in love, deep in your love, oh Sita,
The path to paradise feels incomplete without
you above.
I choose to live on this Earth, here with you by
my side,
Together we'll create our world, a love so pure
and wide.
We'll build our dreams together; hand in hand,
we'll stand,
And in the service of Mother India, we'll uplift
this sacred land.
With you, we'll nurture this nation, give it our
combined might,
For I need no heaven; without you, it lacks light.

It feels incomplete, empty without your
embrace,
And if I must die, let it be in the warmth of your
grace.
Together, we shall reach the gates of heaven so
high,
For even heaven feels incomplete without you
nearby.
I do not seek paradise if you're not there,
With you, my Sita, even the heavens need your
care.

In life and death, in every breath, you are my
world,
For your love, my Sita, makes all the heavens
unfurled.

The Eternal Love of Shiva and Parvati

In the stillness of the mountains, where silence reigns supreme,
Shiva sat in deep meditation, lost in an endless dream.
But then came Parvati, with grace and tender light,
Her love awakened the Lord from his tranquil, cosmic flight.
She, the daughter of the mountains, with a heart so pure and kind,
Saw beyond his ashes, his solitude, his ever-meditative mind.
With patience, she pursued him, unwavering in her devotion,
Her love, like the river's flow, deep with endless emotion.

And Shiva, the great ascetic, who cared for none but time,
Felt his heart stir with her love, in rhythms so sublime.
In her eyes, he found the universe; in her soul, his eternal flame,
Parvati, his Shakti, his world, no longer the same.
Together they danced in the cosmic play of destruction and creation,
Their love, a divine union, the source of all salvation.
She, his equal, his other half, the power behind his might,
With her, he is whole, the day balanced by the night.
Through lifetimes they return, their love forever strong,
In her arms, he finds his home, where he truly does belong.

For Shiva's love for Parvati is eternal, pure, and grand,
Together, they hold the universe in the palm of their hands.

In each heartbeat, in every breath, their love flows endlessly,

The Lord and His beloved, a bond for all
eternity.

The Love of Allah

In the stillness of the night, beneath the starry
dome,
A whisper stirs the heart, calling us back home.
In every breath, in every sigh, His presence we
can feel,
The love of Allah surrounds us, a warmth that's
truly real.
From mountains high to oceans deep, His mercy
flows like streams,
In the beauty of creation, we find hope in our
dreams.
The sun that rises in the east, the moon that
lights the dark,
Each moment is a blessing; each heartbeat holds
His spark.
He sees the tears that fall, the struggles that we
bear,

In the silence of our prayers, He listens with
great care.
For in our darkest hours, when shadows seem to
fall,
The love of Allah guides us, answering our call.
His love is like the gentle breeze that dances
through the trees,
It whispers to our souls, bringing comfort and
ease.
In the laughter of a child, in the bloom of a
flower,
We witness His affection, His never-failing
power.
So let us walk in gratitude; let our hearts sing
His praise,
For the love of Allah sustains us through all our
earthly days.
In unity, we find strength; in faith, we stand as
one,
For His love is the light that guides us till our
journey's done.
With every act of kindness, with every word of
grace,
We reflect His love upon this world, in every
time and place.
So let us cherish this gift; let our spirits soar
above,
In the heart of every believer, there lies the love
of Allah.

The Love of Waheguru

In the quiet of the morning, when the world
begins to wake,
A gentle whisper fills the air—a call we cannot
shake.
It is the love of Waheguru, guiding each step we
take,
In every breath and heartbeat, in every choice we
make.
At the Golden Temple's heart, where peace and
love entwine,
A sacred light illuminates, a presence so divine.
In each prayer and every hymn, we feel His
warm embrace,
The love of Waheguru shines, a light in every
place.
His light shines through the darkness, a beacon
of pure grace,

In moments of confusion, we find our sacred
space.
With open hearts, we seek Him; in the silence,
we find peace,
In the love of Waheguru, our worries find
release.
From Guru Nanak's wisdom to Guru Gobind's
brave fight,
Each Guru leaves a legacy, guiding us to light.
In the teachings of each master, we find our way
to Him,
In the love of Waheguru, our spirits soar and
swim.
The rivers flow with kindness, the mountains
stand so tall,
In nature's vast creation, we hear His loving call.
With every leaf that rustles, with every star
above,
The universe sings praises, reflecting
Waheguru's love.
Through trials and tribulations, His presence
ever near,
In laughter and in sorrow, He wipes away our
fear.
His teachings light the pathway, through the
storm and strife,
In the love of Waheguru, we discover true life.
With every act of service, with every prayer we
share,

We honor all the Gurus, their teachings
everywhere.
In the hearts of all believers, His spirit finds a
home,
In the love of Waheguru, we are never alone.
So let us celebrate this bond, so deep and ever
true,
In unity, we found strength; in gratitude, we
grew.
For the love of Waheguru is the essence of our
being,
In His embrace, we flourish; in His light, we
keep believing.

The Love of Gautama Buddha

In the shade of the Bodhi tree, where silence met the soul,
A seeker found enlightenment, a path to make us whole.
Gautama Buddha, wise and calm, unveiled the sacred truth,
Through compassion and understanding, he sparked the flame of youth.
He taught the Middle Path, a balance of heart and mind,
Not in excess, nor in lack, true peace is what we find.
With every step of mindfulness, he guided weary hearts,
To end the cycle of suffering, a journey that imparts.

His teachings reached great kings, like Ashoka's
mighty reign,
From a warrior to a peacemaker, he broke the
chains of pain.
Ajatashatru learned to lead with mercy as his
guide,
Through Buddha's gentle wisdom, nations
turned the tide.
Ashoka embraced non-violence; his empire
transformed,
In edicts carved on pillars, the seeds of love
were sown.
Ajatashatru, too, found grace, as hatred turned to
care,
In the light of Buddha's teachings, compassion
filled the air.
From royal halls to humble homes, his influence
spread wide,
In every act of kindness, his legacy abides.
For in the hearts of many, his teachings still
inspire,
To live with love and courage, igniting passion's
fire.
In meditation's quiet breath, we hear his voice
today,
A call to seek our inner peace, to find a brighter
way.
Through compassion, he united; in harmony we
stand,

The love of Gautama Buddha still echoes across
the land.
His wisdom guides our leaders as they strive for
what is right,
Injustice met with kindness; in darkness, shines
the light.
So let us walk the Middle Path with hearts both
open wide,
Embracing all beings with love, let kindness be
our guide.
For in this shared existence, we find our truest
aim,
In the love of Gautama Buddha, we ignite the
eternal flame.
His teachings, like a river, flow through time,
forever pure,
In the love of Buddha's essence, we find the path
to cure.

The Love of Mahavir

In the tranquil hills of Girnar, where sacred
whispers flow,
A light of boundless wisdom shone, where only
truth would grow.
Mahavir, the Jain Muni, with purity profound,
Walked the path of sacrifice, where love and
peace abound.
His heart, a vessel of compassion, embraced all
living things,
In silence, he taught forgiveness; in humility, he
sings.
He renounced the earthly treasures for the
wealth of the divine,
In every act of kindness, his spirit would
entwine.

In Palitana's temples, where devotion paints the
air,

Each marble carved with love, a testament laid
bare.
Mount Abu's grandeur rises, with Dilwara's
splendor bright,
Where seekers come to find their peace, in the
soft embrace of light.
With every step he taught us, the value of each
breath,
To see the world as sacred, to honor life, not
death.
Through penance and patience, he forged the
way ahead,
A path of pure compassion where even fear has
fled.
His teachings echo through the ages, a legacy so
rare,
To love without attachment, to nurture, and to
care.
In temples of Rajasthan, where faith is built on
trust,
Mahavir's light still guides us, a beacon bright
and just.
For in the heart of every Jain, his love forever
glows,
A reminder of the purity that only kindness
knows.
In every whispered prayer, in every joyful
chime,

The love of Mahavir endures, transcending
space and time.
So let us walk his path with reverence and grace,
Embracing all existence in this sacred, shared
space.

For in the teachings of Mahavir, we find our
souls' true plea,
To live in love and harmony, to set our spirits
free.

Ode to Devi Saraswati

Oh Devi Saraswati, goddess of wisdom divine,
Your love for your bhakt is a gift so sublime.
With grace, you sit on a swan, pure and bright,
A lotus in your hand, a beautiful sight.
Holding the Vedas, the eternal truth,
And strumming your veena, inspiring the youth.
Your melodies weave through the fabric of time,
In every note and rhythm, we find the divine.
You provide all the knowledge, from ancient to
new,
In every pursuit, we seek guidance from you.
May your love be on me, like a gentle embrace,
To grant me the wisdom to navigate life's race.
From the study of music to the depths of the
mind,
From tantra's rich teachings to silence, so kind.
Guide me through warfare, with strategy clear,
Help me find peace in each moment I'm here.

May your love be bestowed on each child in the
land,
Inspiring bright futures with your nurturing
hand.
Oh Devi Saraswati, shine your light ever near,
In every pursuit of knowledge, let your voice be
clear.
In classrooms and temples, in hearts far and
wide,
Your wisdom empowers, with each thought as
our guide.

Oh Goddess of learning, with compassion so
vast,
Your love is our treasure, a blessing
unsurpassed.
So here I offer my prayer, with sincerity
profound,
In every note I play, in every word I've found.
May your love surround us as we seek and
explore,
Oh Devi Saraswati, we cherish you evermore.

Ode to the Love of Jesus

In a humble stable, under the starry sky,
A child was born, destined to heal and to fly.
With love in His heart, He walked on this Earth,
Teaching kindness and grace, revealing true
worth.
He cured the blind, gave sight to the lost,
With a touch and a word, He cared not for the
cost.
The sick found their solace, the weary found
peace,
In His gentle embrace, their suffering would
cease.
At the wedding in Cana, the miracle was sweet,
With water turned to wine, He made the
celebration complete.
His love flowed like rivers, abundant and free,
A testament to the joy and the heart's jubilee.

Yet the path was not easy; the shadows grew
near,
He bore the world's pain, a burden so dear.
Upon a cruel cross, with nails in His hands,
For the sake of all humanity, He made His last
stands.
With thorns as His crown, He endured every
jeer,
Crucified for our sins, His love crystal clear.
In agony, He suffered; yet His heart was so pure,
Forgiving the lost souls; in His love, we endure.
But love conquers all, and death could not bind,
For on the third day, a miracle we find.
He rose from the grave, transcending mankind,
Alive in our hearts, His spirit entwined.
In a café once more, His presence was felt,
With bread and with wine, our sorrow He dealt.
"Peace be with you," He spoke with a smile,
In the warmth of His love, we linger awhile.
With love unending, He taught us to care,
To love one another in moments all rare.
From the cross to the heavens, His spirit now
soars,
In the hearts of the faithful, His love ever pours.

Ode to the Love of a Pet

In the quiet of dawn, a soft rustle I hear,
A wagging tail greets me, bringing warmth and
cheer.
With eyes bright and gleaming, like stars in the
night,
My furry companion, a true heart's delight.
Oh, how they cuddle, nestling close by my side,
In their gentle embrace, all worries subside.
With a soft, playful nudge and a joyful little
bark,
They fill my days with laughter, lighting up
every dark.
A tiny little whimper, a cute noise they make,
Like music to my soul, for their love never
shakes.
With every wag of their tail and every tender
glance,

I'm reminded of the beauty in this simple
romance.
Through every stormy weather, they stand by
my side,
A bond so unwavering, a love that's my pride.
With soft paws on my lap and a heartbeat so
near,
In their presence, I find solace; in their love, I
feel clear.
They teach me the meaning of loyalty and grace,
In their caring spirit, I find my true place.
With a tilt of their head and a playful little spin,
They remind me of life's joys, how love should
begin.
So here's to the pets, with their hearts open
wide,
In this dance of affection, we take on the ride.
With each wag and purr, every bark and soft
sigh,
In their boundless love, I find my reason to fly.

Together we journey, through thick and thin,
In their gentle warmth, I know I will win.
For the love of a pet is a treasure so true,
A bond that brings joy in all that we do.

Ode to Gaumata: The Sacred Cow

Oh Gaumata, revered and divine,
Your love is infinite; in every heartbeat, you shine.
On the fields of green, you gracefully roam,
In your gentle presence, we find our true home.
You give us milk, pure and white,
A gift from your heart, nourishing delight.
With every drop, you strengthen our bones,
In your nurturing embrace, we've found our own.
Your love is like a mother's, tender and true,
A bond that transcends, forever renewed.
You graze in the meadows, so calm and serene,
A symbol of peace, where life feels like a dream.
With soft, soulful eyes and a spirit so bright,
You teach us compassion, to cherish the light.
In every moo and sigh, a story you share,

Of devotion and grace, a love beyond compare.
Oh Gaumata, sacred and wise,
In your humble presence, our spirits arise.

You enrich our lives in so many ways,
A living reminder to honor and praise.
From ancient scriptures to the hearts of the wise,
You embody the essence of life's sweetest ties.
In the rituals of joy, in festivals grand,
Your love unites us, hand in hand.
So here's to you, Gaumata, beloved and true,
In gratitude, we gather, with reverence anew.
May we honor your spirit in all that we do,
For the love of Gaumata is eternal and true.

Ode to Lord Ganesha: The Remover of Obstacles

Oh Ganesha, oh Ganesha, your love is beyond this universe,
A cosmic embrace that fills our hearts, diverse.
With an elephant face, so gentle and kind,
In your divine presence, true peace we find.
You provide knowledge, wisdom profound,
In every challenge faced, your guidance is found.
With your axe of clarity, ignorance you sever,
Cutting through darkness, leading us ever.
Your goad, a reminder of ethical paths,
Guiding us gently, preventing our wraths.
In every action, may righteousness prevail,
With you as our beacon, we shall not fail.
Your belly, a vessel of nectar so sweet,
Filled with ultimate knowledge, where bliss and wisdom meet.

In the depths of Vedanta, we seek and explore,
With each bite of insight, we hunger for more.
Oh Ganesha, your broken tooth tells a tale,
Of learning from journeys where we sometimes
fail.
In the cracks of experience, wisdom we glean,
Teaching us patience in moments unseen.
Your trunk, a symbol of pure bliss divine,
Discerning truth from falsehood, forever you
shine.
With a gentle sway, you clear our way,
In the dance of life, you guide every day.
Oh Ganesha, oh Ganesha, we honor your grace,
In every prayer whispered, in every sacred
space.
Your love is a tapestry, woven with care,
A reminder of unity, a bond we all share.
So here we stand; in reverence we kneel,
With hearts full of gratitude, your presence we
feel.
May your love guide us in all that we do,
Oh Ganesha, beloved, we worship you true.

Your love for your disciples, unwavering and
bright,
In every heart you touch, you ignite the light.

The Wonder of Solitude

Love to be alone, be alone, be still,
In the quiet, let your restless heart fill.
Why fear the silence, the soft, empty air?
Why are you scared of being alone, unaware?
Being alone grants you the strength to see,
The hidden truths within, wild and free.
In solitude's arms, your mind can take flight,
Guided by whispers, by inner insight.
You may find shadows, you may glimpse the
light,
But through the silence, you will know your
might.
In darkness or dawn, you will come to know,
The depths of your soul where true wisdom
grows.
Alone doesn't mean breaking bonds of the heart,
It's a journey within, where true growth will
start.

While others may laugh and dance and entwine,
You stand with your soul in its sacred design.
For love in your heart begins with your own,
In the stillness, a seed of wonder is sown.
Embrace who you are, in the quiet unknown,
And find that the solitude sharpens your tone.
Be alone, be alone; let your spirit arise,
In the silence, there's magic and wondrous surprise.
A world unfolds within your own mind,
In the beauty of aloneness, peace you will find.
Let the echoes of silence be your guiding song,
In solitude's grace, you find where you belong.
Love yourself deeply, in stillness and grace,
For alone, you'll discover your own sacred space.

The Love of Nothingness

Love of nothingness, a curious thing,
Wonder what nothingness truly brings?
What is this void, this silent abyss,
The origin of how wonderful all is?
It is all about nothing, you see,
But from nothingness springs everything to be.
From the silent shadows where darkness hides,
The mind, the god particle, and desire arise.
For all combined in a divine array,
From planets to ants to beings of clay.
Why fear the stillness, the quiet unknown?
Nothingness births both seed and stone.
From this emptiness, the universe grows,
The place where beginnings and endings both
flow.
Why so scared of the vast, empty space?
That's where it all starts—the cosmic embrace.
From the sound of nothing, "Om" takes flight,

A mantra that shakes the universe with might.
But to feel nothingness, breathe
deep—"Soham,"

It means "I am that," the bright and the calm.
All is bright, all is dark, intertwined,
In nothingness, beginnings and endings align.
For in the stillness, both time and space bend,
Nothingness is where all things begin and end.

Embrace the Love of Nature

Love nature, for it loves you too,
In every breath, in skies so blue.
The wind you feel, the air you take,
It's nature's gift; make no mistake.
The earth beneath, the fire's glow,
The waters calm, the breezes flow.
You are made of these, don't you see?
Air, fire, water, earth, and the sky, so free.
So love nature freely, open your heart,
Let her grace fill every part.
Feel her power as you roam,
In her vast arms, you find your home.
The sun that rises, the moon that shines,
The lakes, the seas, the forest's pines.
All are whispers of nature's grace,
Her gentle touch in every place.
Hey, lovely soul, love nature too,
For you're crafted from her sacred brew.

The air you breathe, the life you feel,
Her elements are what make you real.
Listen close to the water's song,
To the trees that hum where winds belong.
Feel the earth beneath your feet,
In nature's love, you are complete.
And even when this life is through,
Your body returns to what it knew.
Dissolved in nature's grand design,
A sacred bond through space and time.
So love her freely, love her deep,
In her embrace, you wake and sleep.
From birth to death, in her, you stay,
So honor nature, come what may.

The Love of Painting

I love to paint, I love to create,
As colors blend, my soul feels great.
I mix the hues to make my shade,
On a blank canvas, my dreams cascade.
A splurge of strokes, a burst of flame,
From every line, a shape takes aim.
Red, yellow, velvet, white—
They make my painting bold and bright.
Green, orange, blue, and pink,
Add the glow, make hearts rethink.
Oh, the love of painting sets me free,
In silent peace, I let it be.
Through silence, I find solitude,
Where colors speak, soft and shrewd.
From solitude to nothingness, I go,
And that's where my true paintings grow.
The deep shades rise from nature's grace,
A view that lights up every face.

The vibrant tones, the calming blend,
In every stroke, I find my friend.
I love to paint; it makes me whole,
A world of beauty on a scroll.
From nothingness, creation springs,
In every brush, my spirit sings.

The Love of a Book

Love for a book has no words to say,
It sits by your side, come night or day.
A friend so true, with stories to lend,
A book is the best, the truest friend.
No expectation, no anger, no pride,
In the pages of books, there's nothing to hide.
Guilt-free love, no strings to pull,
Each page you turn makes your heart full.
It offers you knowledge, a spark, a clue,
Time passes with glee as it teaches you too.
The smell of its pages, earthy and sweet,
Makes reading a pleasure, a cherished treat.
In moments of need, it's always there,
A friend indeed, beyond compare.
The pages are paper, their scent like a rose,
The words bring peace and a story to a close.
So love a book, take it as a friend,
It asks nothing of you, just time to spend.

No demands, no worries—just stories that blend,
A faithful companion until the end.

Selfless Love for Her

Love for a girl or lady should be free,
A kindness given, like waves in the sea.
Hold her gently; let her fears ease,
And shower her with love, as soft as a breeze.
Pamper her with flowers, in joy's gentle glow,
Love her selflessly; let expectations go.
For love's not a game of want and take,
It's in giving your heart, for her own sake.
Why expect? Why demand? Just give all you've
got,
Like a mother's love, pure and unbought.
Be her friend, be her guide, and be a shoulder to
lean,
In her hardest times, be her unseen sheen.
Clap in her joy and stand through her storm,
If you truly love, keep her spirit warm.
For love without bounds is love divine,
Like Radha's and Krishna's, timeless, fine.

In this world, love like this may be rare,
But if it's real, it needs only care.
Let go of the need, the desire to expect,
And love with a heart that never neglects.
Selfless and true, let your heart unfold,
In love as pure as stories told.
If you truly love, why demand or sigh?
Just love her wholeheartedly and reach for the
sky.
Love for a girl or lady should be free,
A gift unclaimed, as vast as the sea.

Ode to the Motherland

Love your motherland, hold her dear,
With heart and soul, keep her near.
You are born of her soil, her skies so free,
So love her deeply, let your pride be.
Fight for her honor, if duty should call,
Sing for her glory; stand tall for it all.
Dance in her joy, defend her name,
For her pride is ours, her honor, our flame.
But pause a moment and wonder within—
Are these borders we draw where love should
begin?
Wasn't she boundless, ages ago,
A world without borders, where all could flow?
For in a dream, we're one family tree,
A world united, where all are free.
Yet still, I say, love her, your land,
For in that love, we take a stand.
Pride in our roots, in unity's might,

Our motherland brings strength and light.
Let her be whole, not torn by divide,
Where hearts come together and walk side by
side.
So write your stories, spread them wide,
Let no boundary be where love can't reside.
For the love of country, let it expand,
To love Mother Earth, to cherish her land.
Love your motherland, this earth so vast,
A world without limits, free from the past.
As we honor the ground on which we stand,
Let's love Mother Earth, our truest land.

Love Your Mother Deep

Love your mother, love her true,
Her heart beats endlessly just for you.
You may not understand, not till you're grown,
The depths of her love that she's always shown.
She has less time, so cherish her care,
Hold her close, for moments are rare.
As years go by, you'll come to know,
Her wisdom, her worries, how her love flows.
When you're down, her worry's profound,
Her nights grow sleepless as troubles surround.
If ever you're hurt, her tears will fall,
She'd cry forever if she lost you at all.
So love her deeply, ease her fears,
Lift her up through life's tough years.
When she's unwell, be her light,
Your joy alone can make her bright.
Travel with her when health allows,
Capture memories; make her proud.

Gift her laughter, give her grace,
For she has only a little space.
Love your mother each day you're near,
For time is precious, and love is dear.

Love for the Beach

Love for a beach, it's truly a choice,
Where waves sing softly, a calming voice.
As sands shine bright, your hands entwine,
In warm embrace, like a soothing wine.
When water kisses the sunlit sand,
It warms your spirit, soft and grand.
A look from afar, breath catches in line,
With tides that echo, deep as mine.
The sound of waves on rocks below,
Brings peace within, a gentle flow.
With shells and crabs and ocean's song,
The salty breeze feels right along.
Sunrise and sunset, a glorious light,
Colors that paint the day and night.
Love the beach; let it sweep you off your feet,
A slice of heaven, where earth and ocean meet.

What is love for self? Oh, what could it be?

Look deeper, look deeper—set your spirit free.
Is love for self a love for truth?
Or a journey within to uncover youth?
Look inside, go on, take the dive,
For the love of self makes the spirit thrive.
In the silence, in that quiet grace,
Self-realization finds its place.
Looking inside, you'll meet pure emptiness,
Where from nothingness springs all fullness.
So love yourself, dive, and explore,
Look inside, look deeper; there's more.
Beneath the clouds of thought, go steep,
Where vibrant truths begin to seep.
Clear away clouds, the vibrant self will rise,
Yet inside that self, no substance lies.
In that nothing lies answers above,
To all the mysteries of self-love.

So look inside, look inside—don't hide,
Find self-love by looking deep inside.

Love Your Sadguru Deep

Love your Sadguru, love him true,
For he'll break the slumber encasing you.
He'll awaken your life, bring clarity fine,
And guide you to paths where souls intertwine.
Life's meant for awareness, not shallow dreams,
He'll teach you to live where consciousness
beams.
In trials or peace, he'll stand by your side,
Through the ups and downs of life's wild ride.
To the penultimate, your Sadguru will show,
But it's up to you to let wisdom grow.
He alone reveals life's secret goal—
Self-realization, the journey of the soul.
So love him deeply, trust his way,
For he'll lead you beyond, to a brighter day.
With His grace, the ultimate truth you'll find,
Moksha awaits with a peaceful mind.
Love him deeply, love him true,
For freedom and wisdom, he'll gift to you.

Love for Human Birth

Love that you're human, this gift so rare,
Countless lives behind to bring you here.
If you study deep, your soul will steep,
In the wisdom of forms, you had to reap.
Don't waste this birth; let purpose unfurl,
Find your Sadguru; seek wisdom's pearl.
Life's true goal is knowing the self,
Beyond chasing power, status, or wealth.
Surrender pride, wealth, and lust,
At the feet of wisdom, learn to trust.
For in the end, when we pass on,
Only karma stays; our deeds live on.
You came with nothing; you'll leave the same,
Karmic echoes are all that remain.
Small as a molecule in this grand design,
What's there in pride? Let your ego decline.
Don't chase money, don't chase fame,
For self-realization is life's only aim.

Be wise, be wise, look within,
Query your soul; let growth begin.
Understand that the self is vast, yet nothing at all,
Only by looking inward can illusions fall.
So love this human birth; it's a chance to see
The depths within, life's true mystery.

Love by Children

Love by children, so genuine, so pure,
A gift from the heart that will always endure.
They say children are a form of God,
Innocent souls, on life's bright path they trod.
Pure at heart, without pride or shame,
No ego to carry, no guilt to tame.
They pour their love without reserve,
In each little gesture, pure and uncurved.
They make you a card or cook you a meal,
With small hands busy, their love so real.
They offer their treasures with a generous heart,
Their love untainted, a work of art.
So be gentle with them; give love in return,
Hug them close, for these moments will burn
Bright in your heart as time goes by—
When their love was pure as the endless sky.
Listen to them, spend some time,
These years of innocence, a brief climb.

For soon they'll grow, no longer so small,
And you'll miss that love, the purest of all.

Ode to Devi Lakshmi

Oh Lakshmi, oh Lakshmi, goddess so divine,
I bow to you and send my love, in every line.
Oh, Lakshmi, oh Lakshmi, in all you bestow,
Grant peace and joy; let all life's blessings flow.
I pray you to make every soul prosperous and
bright,
Where you dwell, there shines endless light.
Where there is cleanliness, prosperity reigns,
Where knowledge flows, wisdom gains.
Where there is strength, success is near,
Where art is cherished, joy appears.
Your grace brings abundance and radiant peace,
May your blessings in every home increase.
I bow to Vishnu's heart, where you reside,
At his feet, where you eternally abide.
Oh, Vishnu Priya, to you, I surrender my all,
With devotion so deep, in your name, I call.
With lotus in hand, prosperity flows,

Your gifts, like rivers, for all to know.
You hold the keys to life's sacred aim,
Dharma, Artha, Kama, and Moksha's flame.
Oh, Devi Lakshmi, I pray you to bless this age,
With wisdom and wealth on every page.
In your love, I feel both mother and guide,
Accept me, your child, in my humble stride.
I greet you, Devi, with love so sweet,
At your pious feet, I lay my prayer complete.
Bless every heart with joy and peace,
Oh Lakshmi, let your blessings never cease.

Love Your Father, Love Him Strong

Love your father, love him strong,
For he's been your strength all along.
He hides his heart, his love concealed,
But every care for you revealed.
In silence, he stands, emotions kept tight,
Yet in your joy, he finds his light.
He holds you up when you may fall,
And cheers you on through it all.
From childhood days to growing years,
He's walked beside, through hopes and fears.
He may not ask, may need no gift,
But in his giving, he finds his lift.
In his old age, when he's grown weak,
Give him your care, the love he seeks.
Remember his strength, the arms so strong,
Now it's your turn to help him along.
For there may come a time when he's frail,

But love him then; let not your love fail.
Love your father, love him deep,
In his heart, such memories keep.

The Love for Travel, the Love for Sight

Love travel, love travel, roam near and far,
Each journey, each step, a fresh guiding star.
You explore new places, meet someone new,
And in their stories, find insights too.
In each new face, a world's delight,
In each new land, a spark ignites.
See new cultures, taste their spice,
In all these wonders, wisdom lies.
Seek solace in kingdoms vast and grand,
Across Europe, America, Japan's fair land.
Travel India, oceans wide,
With an open heart and an open mind.
From temples high to mosques of grace,
Churches, monasteries—a holy place.
Beaches, museums, and mountains tall,
Let no barrier keep you small.
Yet ponder this: does travel alone

Bring peace, or make the soul your home?
For even in stillness, the journey is deep,
When you close your eyes, new worlds you meet.
So wander freely, roam with zeal,
But know the peace within is real.
For every path brings you back home,
To grasp it all and seek your own.
Return at dusk, from lands wide,
Come and grasp it all, then look inside.

Love Your Food, Love to Share

Love your food, love each bite,
Eat what you love; make each meal bright.
Sometimes what you crave is hard to get,
So cherish each morsel with no regret.
Try new flavors, cuisines so fine,
In every dish, let your spirit shine.
Love your food, but sharing's the art,
For giving from the heart is where kindness
starts.
If you earn enough to spare,
Share your food; show that you care.
For while your plate may overflow,
Others hunger, as you well know.
You may have many, some just one,
So share a morsel; let kindness be done.
Remember Bhishma's timeless tale,
When Yudhishthira's act did prevail.

In that lesson, the Kauravas learned,
That a meal's true worth is in love earned.
So love, value, and pass it along,
Sharing food is where we all belong.
The mantra stands: love, value, share,
In every bite, let kindness be there.

Love Your Health, Treasure the Wealth

Love your health, for it is gold,
A priceless gift as we grow old.
Health is wealth, wise ones say,
Guard it well, each passing day.
You may have pride, riches, and fame,
But without your health, it's just a name.
Do Surya Namaskar, breathe in deep,
Do pranayama; your soul will keep.
Or run, lift weights, or stretch and tone,
In every movement, health is grown.
Exercise is wealth in disguise,
For a healthy body makes you wise.
Eat with care, make choices right,
For health's the goal in every bite.
Being healthy in body and mind,
Is where wisdom and peace you'll find.
A healthy heart, a calm, clear head,

Is worth more than riches or bread.
With strength in body, spirit, and soul,
Health makes you ready to reach every goal.
So greet each dawn with work on self,
For today's the treasure, today's the wealth.
Yesterday's gone, tomorrow's a dream,
But today's the day to build your esteem.
Do Surya Namaskar, do yoga's art,
Or take up weights with a steady heart.
Love your health, for in life's test,
A healthy life is truly blessed.

Love All Beings, Embrace the Whole

Love all beings, hold them dear,
From the smallest ant to those we revere.
In this vast universe, so grand and wide,
We're but tiny specks, with no place for pride.
Love everyone, from the smallest to tall,
For we are connected, each one, to all.
With open hearts, no judgment or strings,
Let love be the freedom that our spirit brings.
Bow to the Divine in each living soul,
With love that is boundless, pure, and whole.
Love without expectation; just let it be,
For love, like water, sets us free.
Even the gods bow down to love's might,
In Bhakti's glow, their spirits delight.
For in the Bhagavad Gita, paths unfold—
Karma, Bhakti, Knowledge bold.
In Bhakti's embrace, love's flame grows,

And with it, divine purpose shows.
Love all beings, release every tie,
Through love, transcend, and reach the sky.
Love your mother, father, wife,
Gurus, friends who share your life.
Love without bounds, from deep inside,
This path alone brings joy and pride.
Look within to love all kind,
And step beyond what holds the mind.
Through this love, moksha awaits,
Breaking free from earthly weights.
Take God's name, embrace it tight,
This love will guide you through the night.
Love all beings, pure and true,
And in this love, find freedom anew.
From the smallest ant to the human heart,
We're all connected; each plays a part.
So love all beings, one and all,
And find in love, life's greatest call.